MOUNTAIN LIONS

Jack Ballard

GUILFORD, CONNECTICUT
HELENA, MONTANA

This book is dedicated to the hope that mountain lions may once again roam at least some of their historic habitat in the midwestern and eastern regions of the United States.

FALCONGUIDES®

An imprint of Rowman & Littlefield
Falcon, FalconGuides, and Outfit Your Mind are registered trademarks of Rowman & Littlefield.

Distributed by NATIONAL BOOK NETWORK

Copyright © 2015 by Rowman & Littlefield

Photos by Jack Ballard unless otherwise noted. NPS photos courtesy of the National Park Service, USFWS photos courtesy of the US Fish and Wildlife Service.

British Library Cataloguing-in-Publication Information Available

Library of Congress Cataloging-in-Publication Data

Ballard, Jack (Jack Clayton)
  Mountain lions / Jack Ballard.
     pages cm
  Includes index.
  ISBN 978-1-4930-1255-8 (pbk.) — ISBN 978-1-4930-1437-8 (e-book) 1. Puma. I. Title.
  QL737.C23B2627 2015
  599.75'24—dc23
                           2015019778

∞™ The paper used in this publication meets the minimum requirements of American National Standard for Information Sciences—Permanence of Paper for Printed Library Materials, ANSI/NISO Z39.48-1992.

Contents

Chapter 6: Mountain Lions and Humans

Acknowledgments

Much effort has been expended in recent years in mountain lion research. I am indebted to all the researchers who have advanced our understanding of these intriguing creatures. Two reference works were found to be extremely helpful: *Cougar: Ecology and Conservation*, edited by Maurice Hornocker and Sharon Negri, and *Desert Puma: Evolutionary Ecology and Conservation of an Enduring Carnivore*. Anyone wanting to better understand cougars would do well to read these works. Special thanks goes to Marilyn Cuthill of Beringia South, one of the leading mountain lion research centers in the United States, for reviewing and making helpful comments on the manuscript.

Swarovski Optics generously provided superb binoculars to aid my field observations of wildlife. Thank you!

Introduction

The cry was startling and chilling. Laden with a backpack and grinding up a wilderness trail with my older brother in late November, we heard what sounded like a woman screaming in a grove of quaking aspens adjacent to the path. Although the noise was new to my ears, I recognized it immediately as the scream of a mountain lion. We camped about a mile up the trail. Remembering that spine-tingling wail, we had a hard time falling asleep that night.

In all likelihood we witnessed the call of a female looking for a mate, as mountain lions may mate at any time of the year. The unnerving experience lingered in my consciousness for the duration of our outing, but I knew we were in little danger from the vocalizing cat. Mountain lions infrequently attack humans. Such incidences are very rare—so much so that we were at greater risk of a fatality while driving to the trailhead than succumbing to the claws and jaws of a cougar.

Beyond hearing that eerie call, my experiences with mountain lions, in four decades of tramping the wildlands of America, have been surprisingly few. I have discovered the tracks of cougars on several occasions. I have sighted a mountain lion but twice. A friend and I observed a large male dart in front of my pickup on a mountain road at dawn. The animal paused in the evergreens for a few moments, giving us a clear, but brief view of its massive paws and muscular body. Another time, I caught the outline of four animals on the highway in my headlights before daylight. They appeared about the size of wolves. I slowed in anticipation of a pack sighting. Instead, my headlights illuminated a female mountain lion with three nearly grown kittens. The youngsters continued to romp for a moment, their presence and antics bringing a broad smile to my face. But their mother quickly shepherded them to the roadside, a matron apparently not quite ready to leave her offspring unsupervised.

As I write this while sitting at Chicago's O'Hare Airport, the image of a seated mountain lion greets me from the tail of a

Frontier Airlines plane. It appears a sub-adult, its intelligent amber eyes seemingly captivated by my typing form. Here's hoping this book will similarly captivate the reader with the secret lives of mountain lions, and enhance, if even in small measure, our society's respect and toleration for these enigmatic cats.

Chapter 1 Names and Faces

Names and Visual Description

Mountain lion is the name given to a large wild member of the cat family in North America. The name, however, is somewhat misleading. Members of this species can thrive in deserts and woodlands as well as the mountains. Historically, and in various regions of the country, the mountain lion has been given many other names, including *cougar*, *puma*, *catamount*, and *panther*. Less frequently the mountain lion has been called the *mountain screamer* or *painter*. There is perhaps no other species in America described by so many monikers. The *Guinness Book of World Records* claims that the mountain lion has the most number of names of any species on Earth. More than forty different names have been given to this feline hunter. In this book, the names mountain lion and cougar will be used interchangeably for variety and in acknowledgement that both terms are often used in scientific and popular literature.

Even the cat's scientific name can be confusing. Mountain lions were scientifically named *Felis concolor* by Carl Linnaeus, the father of modern taxonomy, in the late 1700s. In the 1970s, researchers concluded that mountain lions were not part of the *Felis* genus, which includes housecats and other small wildcats. The mountain lion now shares the *puma* lineage with the cheetah and jaguarundi and is scientifically known as *Puma concolor*, although the former name, *Felis concolor*, still occurs in some scientific and popular literature. The change in the scientific name from *Felis concolor* to *Puma concolor* was officially recognized by the American Society of Mammologists in 1993.

One of the mountain lion's physical characteristics can be inferred from its scientific name. *Concolor* refers to something that exhibits a uniform color. A mountain lion's coat displays a range of hues, depending on where the cat is found, but mountain lions are notably uniform in color. The cat's shades may range

The *concolor* portion of the mountain lion's scientific name refers to the uniform color of its coat. This cat was photographed in Wyoming's Grand Teton National Park. NPS Photo

from tawny red to tawny gray to a rich medium brown. Lighter fur typically adorns its ears and cheeks and the inside of its legs and belly. A small black patch of fur is found at the tip of the tail, and the animal sports black stripes or irregular spots on the muzzle, sometimes referred to as a moustache.

Mountain lions look somewhat like an enormous, lean, athletic housecat. Their eyes are large and usually appear yellowish or hazel in color, although very young mountain lions have blue eyes. A cougar's ears are fairly short and rounded at the tips. The animals sport a nose pad that may vary from pink to brown (sometimes with black spots) and long, pale whiskers. In relation to its body, the legs of a mountain lion are quite long. Its legs appear rather thick and muscular. One of the most distinguishing physical characteristics of the mountain lion is its very long, full tail. It often accounts for nearly 40 percent of the animal's total length, and the cat carries its tail in a drooping or lowered position while walking or standing motionless.

The terminology used to describe the genders and ages of cats in the cougar family varies. It is sometimes similar to that used to describe housecats. Domestic male cats are called *toms*, female housecats are officially known as *mollies*, or *queens* if they are nursing young. Baby or immature housecats are dubbed *kittens*. In scientific literature, the genders of mountain lions are usually referred to simply as *males* and *females*. The young are often called *kittens*, although scientific literature may also refer to them as *cubs* or simply

Baby mountain lions are called *kittens* or *cubs*. A researcher at the Santa Monica Mountain National Recreation Area in California holds this one. NPS Photo

young. Some researchers occasionally call male mountain lions *toms* and the folks who live in cougar country frequently call the animals *tom*. The term *molly* or *queen*, however, does not appear to be part of the common or scientific verbiage associated with mountain lions. Thus, the terminology used to identify the ages and genders of mountain lions can be quite variable, depending on the purpose (scientific versus popular discussion) and place.

Related Species in North America

Mountain lions are one of seven species of wildcats found north of Mexico on the North American continent. They are joined in many places by populations of feral (domestic animals gone wild) housecats that prey upon native birds and small mammals in destructively high numbers.

Genetically, mountain lions are most closely related to the jaguarundi, a small cat whose range occurs from Central America, through Mexico, and is rarely found in the extreme southeastern portions of Texas and New Mexico. Like the mountain lion, the jaguarondi displays solid coloration across its body. The jaguarondi exhibits three distinct colors: black, gray, and reddish. Jaguarundis have long tails, but it is unlikely that a competent observer would confuse them for a mountain lion. An adult jaguarundi weighs from around fifteen to eighteen pounds, roughly seven to ten times smaller than the typical adult mountain lion.

The other five species of wildcats found north of Mexico are all readily distinguished from the mountain lion in appearance as well as size. All of these are spotted to some extent, in contrast to the uniform coloration of the mountain lion and jaguarundi. The largest of these is the jaguar, a stocky spotted cat that may be infrequently found in Texas, New Mexico, and Arizona. The jaguar is the third-largest cat in the world behind the lion and tiger. It is somewhat larger than a mountain lion (perhaps 20 percent larger, on average), although the size of adult mountain lions and jaguars includes considerable overlap. Like cougars, jaguars have

Cougars are slightly smaller than jaguars, although their size overlaps considerably. The spotted jaguar is nearly extinct in the United States. Licensed by Shutterstock.com

4

a long tail. However, the intense dark spotting on their yellowish-gold coats (observable at close range even on the minority population of jaguars with black coats) easily differentiates them from mountain lions.

Two other spotted cats, the margay and the ocelot, are native to the extreme southwestern portions of the United States. The margay is exceedingly rare in the United States if it exists at all. Margays are small cats (around fifteen to twenty pounds) with pronounced spots and long tails. Ocelots range in a limited area in south Texas and are infrequently sighted in southern Arizona. The ocelot is a medium-size wildcat that weighs from twenty to forty pounds. Skilled climbers, ocelots may kill birds roosting in trees. They are beautifully spotted, have fairly long tails, and have been described at times as dwarf leopards.

The paw prints of mountain lions comingle much more frequently with the final two species of North American cats found in the United States: the bobcat and the lynx. Along with their sometimes-spotted coats, bobcats and lynx have other physical characteristics that easily distinguish them from mountain lions. While the grayish lynx may exhibit few distinct spots, its tail is much shorter than the mountain lion's, appearing as a stubby appendage rather than a long, elegant adornment. The ears of lynx are pointed, with distinct tufts of black hair extending from the tip of each ear. Lynx are much smaller than mountain lions. The largest male lynx weighs only around 50 percent of a small mountain lion female. Lynx share habitat with cougars in much of Canada and portions of the northern Rocky Mountains in the United States.

Bobcats are more brownish in color and more heavily spotted than lynx. Like lynx, they have a short stubby tail that looks very different from the long, obvious tail of the mountain lion. Bobcats have pointed ears with black tufts on the tips that are much smaller than those found on the lynx. Bobcats are pint-size in comparison to mountain lions. While some very large males may weigh forty pounds, most bobcats weigh less than thirty pounds, making them much smaller than mountain lions. Bobcats range

Bobcats are the most common feline neighbor to mountain lions in the United States. Their short tail, smaller size, and spots make them easy to distinguish from cougars.
Licensed by Shutterstock.com

across most of the contiguous United States, so they are the cat with which the cougar shares the most extensive part of its range.

Subspecies

Categorizing the various subspecies of mountain lions is fraught with the same questions and controversies that surround attempts to classify the subspecies of many other animals. A subspecies is generally defined as a geographically isolated population of a particular species that displays physical and/or behavioral characteristics that distinguish it from other members of its kind. During the eighteenth and much of the nineteenth centuries, wildlife biologists seemed happy to identify as many subspecies for a particular animal as possible. These were often determined not only on the basis of geography, but on physical attributes such as overall size or variations in skull measurements. Subsequent analysis has questioned many subspecies definitions. For example, the size of an animal is largely determined by the amount and quality of the food sources it has available during its growth years. Thus, a population of bobcats in one vicinity may be 20 percent larger on average than those from a population 100 miles away. In the heyday of subspecies classification, this might constitute the designation of the two as separate subspecies. However, if one population has access to a larger and more stable prey base, the difference in size simply may be a function of nutrition, not true variation in the animals' characteristics. The current trend has thus been toward reducing rather than increasing the number of subspecies identified within a particular animal species.

Another factor at work in present-day "subspecies theory" is the use of DNA analysis. Many biologists feel that genetic kinship established through DNA analysis is more definitive in classifying a subspecies than variation in physical or behavioral characteristics. Thus, subspecies designations based on extensive DNA research usually undergo a re-classification that more closely aligns with the animals' genetic similarities than with the characteristics formerly used to identify the subspecies.

These trends are readily apparent in subspecies classifications for mountain lions. Various biologists from the eighteenth to the twentieth centuries identified as many as thirty-four different subspecies of cougars ranging across North, Central, and South America. Thirteen of those subspecies were identified in North America north of Mexico.

More recently many leading mountain lion biologists, informed by the most current DNA analysis, have reduced the number of subspecies from over thirty to six. Defined genetically, these six subspecies have much larger geographical ranges than previous designations. Of the six subspecies, four are found in South America, a single subspecies exists in Central America, and all of the cougars in North America are grouped together as a single subspecies.

However, as late as 2011 the US Fish and Wildlife Service (USFWS) was still managing mountain lions under the 1946 subspecies classifications proposed by researchers Young and Goldman, who identified fifteen subspecies of mountain lions in North America. Although the USFWS has acknowledged problems with Young and Goldman's subspecies definitions (at least one subspecies was identified on traits associated with the analysis of the skulls of just eight animals), it has yet to formally accept a more recent paradigm of mountain lion subspecies.

Physical Characteristics

Mountain lions inhabit an astonishingly large range from northern British Columbia in North America to the southernmost regions of South America. Due to the variety of habitats over which they roam, mountain lions vary considerably in size. In biological circles, Bergmann's Rule states that within a species, animals are larger on average as one moves from the equator toward the poles. Although this postulate does not apply to all species, it

Mountain lions living in colder climates at latitudes farther from the equator tend to be larger than their kin in warmer climates. Licensed by Shutterstock.com

appears to generally hold true for cougars. On average, the cats are larger in the colder, more extreme climates toward the northern reaches of their range in North America and in the southern parts of their range in South America.

What accounts for this trend? Greater body mass is advantageous in maintaining warmth in the winter, although it also takes more fuel to sustain a larger body. Many of the mountain lion's major sources of food are large ungulates such as mule deer, whitetail deer, and elk. All of these animals tend to follow Bergmann's Rule, with body size for both species of deer increasing substantially toward the northern portions of their range. For predators such as the mountain lion, Bergmann's Rule may simply be a function of killing efficiency. Where prey is larger, predators possessing greater size and strength have an advantage. Thus, mountain lions in the north may simply be larger because they routinely prey on larger animals than their southern cousins.

Mountain lions display a high degree of sexual dimorphism, a term that refers to species in which there is considerable difference in size between males and females. Adult males (animals older than two years of age) are generally around 40 percent heavier than equivalent females. In some smaller populations the variation in average male and female weights may be even more extreme. Researchers in the San Andres Mountains of New Mexico who studied cougars over a ten-year period found that males in the study area were 70 percent heavier on average than females.

Adult female mountain lions typically range from around 75 to 135 pounds. Males normally weigh from 115 to 200 pounds. Occasionally males reach heavier weights. An eviscerated (internal organs removed) male in Arizona was recorded in 1926 as weighing 275 pounds. President Theodore Roosevelt shot a tom weighing a reputed 227 pounds northwest of Meeker, Colorado, in February 1901. Suffice it to say that any male weighing over 200 pounds is on the extreme end of the scale. Female mountain lions are generally 5 to 6 feet in body length with a tail measuring from 21 to 32 inches. Males measure from 5.5 to 9 feet in body length, with tails ranging from 26 to 35 inches. Height measured at the

THE FLORIDA PANTHER

The Florida panther, *Puma concolor coryi*, is one of the subspecies of mountain lions in the United States still recognized by the USFWS and many biologists. Prior to European settlement, mountain lions left their fuzzy paw prints across most of the southeastern United States. By 1900, cougars had been widely eliminated, primarily due to direct eradication through hunting and trapping or indirectly by habitat destruction. However, a small population of the cats persisted in undeveloped areas of south Florida.

The Florida panther was given protection under the Endangered Species Act (ESA) in 1973. At that time the animal's total population in the wild was estimated at just a few dozen individuals. Intensive conservation efforts in the following decades failed to bolster the population. By the 1990s it became apparent that the critically small population was suffering from inbreeding, which caused genetic and physical defects that decreased reproduction. After considerable debate, the population was augmented with eight female mountain lions from Texas in 1995 to promote genetic diversity.

The introduction of genetically dissimilar females appears to have been perhaps a lifesaving measure for the Florida panther. Current population censuses indicate some 100 to 180 of the elusive cats now track the swamps and forests of south Florida, with several refuge areas containing the cat that was designated as the state animal in 1982. Major refuges harboring these mountain lions include Big Cypress National Preserve, the Florida Panther National Wildlife Refuge, and Everglades National Park.

Did the introduction of the eight females (which essentially doubled the number of females in the population) from a different subspecies effectively nullify the Florida panther's status as a subspecies? The USFWS argues it did not. Many independent biologists believe otherwise, some suggesting the Florida panther has never been a legitimate subspecies, simply an isolated population of North American mountain lions that developed genetic and physical peculiarities (such as a kinked tail and cowlick on the back) due to inbreeding. The American public, I suspect, doesn't care. We're just happy these notable animals have maintained a stronghold in the southeast from which, perhaps, their kind may expand into other areas.

Florida panthers roam the forests and swamps of south Florida. They are the only population of cougars that has survived since presettlement times east of the Mississippi River. USFWS Photo

A mountain lion's claws are retractable. Claw marks are not visible on mountain lion tracks. NPS Photo

top of the front shoulder typically ranges from 21 to 30 inches for males. Female shoulder height varies from 17 to 26 inches.

Like housecats, mountain lions have very sharp retractable claws. This feature helps skilled observers distinguish their paw prints from other species, such as bears and wolves. Viewed in snow, mud, or soft soil, cougar prints lack the noticeable claw and toenail marks accompanying the spoor of bears and canines.

Chapter 2

Range and Habitat

Historic Range

The mountain lion's historic range is larger than that of any other land-dwelling animal in the Western Hemisphere (except for humans). Prior to European settlement, cougars were found from northern British Columbia to the southernmost reaches of South America. Their range spanned from the Atlantic Ocean to the Pacific Ocean on both the North and South American continents. In North America, the mountain lion's historic range found its northern limits at a line drawn from roughly the northern border of British Columbia to the southern end of Hudson Bay, then directly eastward to the Atlantic Ocean. South of that line,

Mountain lions require terrain and cover allowing them to successfully stalk prey. This cat was photographed hunting in Glacier National Park, Montana. NPS Photo

cougars are thought to have occupied essentially the entirety of both continents.

However, the existence or abundance of mountain lions in certain parts of this extensive range is uncertain. Cougars are very flexible predators, but a viable prey base is essential to their survival. Even where a prey base is present, competition with other, more formidable predators such as wolf packs or grizzly bears may limit mountain lion numbers. Thus, it is doubtful that mountain lions were ever abundant on the open prairies, where they would no doubt come into conflict with wolves and grizzly bears. Areas that likely contained the greatest number of cougars on the plains included river corridors and other habitat niches that offered trees and cover where mountain lions could elude rival predators and females could safely hide young.

Current Range

The mountain lion's historic range in the Americas has been reduced by nearly half over the past 200 years. South American mountain lions still roam over much of the continent. Their range on the southern continent has retracted to the greatest extent in areas of intense agriculture and where urbanization has occurred. For the most part, these areas include coastal regions on the east and west sides of the continent. The mountain lion's range has also diminished in Central America. The status of mountain lion populations in South and Central America, however, is uncertain. Some biologists have estimated that up to 40 percent of the mountain lion's historic habitat has been negatively altered by urbanization and deforestation. Government management and monitoring of cougar populations are variable. Mountain lions have no legal protection in Ecuador. They are hunted in Mexico and Peru. In other South and Central American countries, they are legally protected, although it is believed they are often still killed in rural areas where they may be a real or perceived threat to livestock.

In the United States, the distribution of cougars has been cut by about two-thirds since prior to European settlement. The mountain lion's range now occurs primarily in the western portion of the United States. The exception to this rule is the Florida panther (the isolated population of cougars in Florida discussed in chapter 1), which is found in the extreme southern portion of Florida. More precisely, Florida panthers are found in portions of nine counties, with Collier County and Miami-Dade Counties claiming the largest segments of habitat. The mountain lion's range in Florida can generally be described as the part of the state south of a line drawn from Fort Myers (Lee County) to the southern end of Lake Okeechobee (Palm Beach County) and west of a line sketched from the south end of Lake Okeechobee to the point at which Highway 1 passes from the mainland to the Florida Keys (Miami-Dade County). The central portion of this approximate distribution holds the highest numbers of Florida panthers.

The rest of the mountain lion's range in the United States occurs far west of Florida, with most of the cougar's range occurring west of the eastern front of the Rocky Mountains. The eastern edge of the mountain lion's range occurs roughly at a boundary drawn from the Canadian border traveling south through the western half of Montana, continuing south through the western

Mountain lions, like this one lounging in the shade in Big Bend National Park, Texas, thrive in arid environments where prey is present. NPS Photo—Reine Wonite

two thirds of Wyoming and Colorado, south along the eastern border of New Mexico, and from the southeastern corner of New Mexico to the Mexico border about 100 miles southeast of Laredo, Texas.

Although the portion of the country that lies west of the boundary outlined here is typically described as mountain lion range on a map of the United States, the extent to which cougars actually inhabit this area is quite variable. For example, the foothills ranching and farming community west of Three Forks, Montana, in which I grew up is included as mountain lion range. However, cougars were unknown to the area in my childhood some forty years ago. Today, mountain lion scat or tracks are rarely sighted in the area, and when they are, they probably come from young cats dispersing from occupied habitat. There really is no resident population. The situation is similar in Washington State and elsewhere. The entire state of Washington is included in current mountain lion range, yet the odds of cats actually colonizing places like the eastern portion of the state, with its intensive agriculture and absence of forests or other cover, are unlikely. Of that massive range through which mountain lions may occasionally travel, perhaps 50 percent is continuously inhabited by these secretive tawny cats.

Beyond the western range described here, mountain lions occupy several areas to the east. In Montana, cougars have reclaimed and continue to expand into other areas of their historic range in a region known as the Missouri Breaks. The Missouri Breaks are an extensive system of badlands, often sprinkled with ponderosa pine trees and junipers along the Missouri River in eastern Montana. Lewis and Clark regularly encountered grizzly bears and bighorn sheep on their epic westward journey in the Missouri Breaks. And it was here that they made their first observation of a mountain lion. The region is currently home to substantial herds of elk and mule deer, with smaller numbers of whitetail deer and bighorn sheep also tracking the deep coulees and forested benches above the river. All of these ungulates represent favored prey for mountain lions.

By the 1930s, mountain lions were eradicated from the Missouri Breaks, their population in Montana restricted to mountainous regions west of the Continental Divide and in the Absaroka-Beartooth region of southwestern Montana. Cougars began expanding their range in the state by 1950, primarily in an eastward direction. The Missouri Breaks were naturally recolonized by the mobile felines by 1990. Mountain lions are also now found in southeastern Montana, primarily in remote timbered areas where deer and elk are also present.

Another nuclear population of mountain lions is located to the east of their primary western range in North Dakota. These animals roam a rugged area in the far western portion of the state often referred to as the "Badlands." The Badlands are found in the south to south-central part of North Dakota, just east of its border with Montana. Cougars were never officially listed as extinct in North Dakota, although the status of the cats in the state throughout most of the twentieth century was uncertain. By 1990, mountain lion observations had become more common, and in 2005 the state began a hunting season for cougars. North Dakota's small mountain lion population has declined in recent years, most likely as a result of too many adult animals being killed during the hunting season.

Some 150 miles to the south, a nuclear population of mountain lions occurs in the Black Hills of South Dakota. The mountainous, timbered topography of the Black Hills provides fine habitat for mountain lions, replete with a diverse array of prey including elk, deer, and many smaller mammals. Mountain lions were listed as a threatened species by the state of South Dakota in 1978. Their numbers increased through the latter part of the 1900s, with the first confirmed kitten born in 1999. Researchers have documented breeding male mountain lions in the Black Hills that have immigrated considerable distances from the Bighorn Mountains (northwestern Wyoming) and the Laramie and Snowy Mountains (southeastern Wyoming). Like the isolated population in North Dakota, it appears that overhunting is currently the most serious threat to the Black Hills population.

The rugged Black Hills of South Dakota are home to a sizeable but isolated population of mountain lions. LISA BALLARD

Two other very small populations of mountain lions persisting east of the major portion of their North American range are worthy of note. A tiny, but reproducing number of mountain lions occurs in the Pine Ridge region of northwestern Nebraska. This small community of cats may hold as few as twenty adults. About 50 miles north of the Montana-Canada border, a breeding population of mountain lions has reestablished itself in the Cypress Hills Interprovincial Park that straddles the Saskatchewan-Alberta border. Mountain lions appeared in the park around the dawn of the third millennium. A viable, slowly expanding population is now found in the park, where they are protected from hunting.

Mountain Lion Habitat

Along with their distinction of occupying the largest range of any terrestrial (land-dwelling) mammal in the Western Hemisphere, it might also be argued that mountain lions occupy the most

Mountain lions are flexible predators capable of living in nearly any ecosystem in North, Central, and South America. Licensed by Shutterstock.com

diverse types of habitat. Historically, mountain lions were found at elevations stretching from sea level to around 15,000 feet. School-children in both the United States and Europe are introduced to the concept of separating various geographic areas that support different types of plant and animal life into units. In America these are known as *biomes*. In Europe they are usually referred to as *major life zones*. Biomes may be labeled as temperate deciduous forests, interior grasslands, tropical rain forests, alpine tundra, and the like. It is believed that as late as 1900, mountain lions inhab-ited every biome in North, Central, and South America, except the arctic tundra.

Two factors dictate where mountains lived historically and continue to persist. Their habitat must support a sufficient prey base that provides sustenance for adult mountain lions, females raising kittens, and sub-adult individuals learning to hunt on their own. This normally includes hoofed animals such as elk and deer,

MOVING EAST?

The successful recolonization of areas such as the Badlands of North Dakota and the Black Hills of South Dakota has many mountain lion enthusiasts speculating about if and when *Puma concolor* might reclaim range even farther east. Questions of cougars in the East have engaged the minds of many. Hundreds of mountain lion sightings are reported in states from Wisconsin to New York each year. Is it possible that a remnant population of the subspecies *Puma concolor couguar* remains in existence?

It appears not. In 2011 the USFWS declared the Eastern cougar extinct and recommended the subspecies be removed from the Endangered Species List under which it had been protected since 1973. The USFWS's review of purported evidence of mountain lions east of the Mississippi River concluded that the vast majority were actually sightings of other creatures such as bobcats or domestic dogs. In cases where mountain lions were actually discovered, the USFWS concluded via DNA analysis that the animals were dispersers from western populations or domestic cougars (typically from South or Central America) that had escaped or been set free by their owners.

Nonetheless, multiple instances of young mountain lions wandering from western enclaves (typically the Black Hills) have been documented in locations such as Wisconsin, Illinois, Nebraska, and Missouri. What are the odds of the cats establishing a breeding population east of their current range?

In terms of habitat, there are numerous places where mountain lions might find a home in the Midwest and eastern regions of the nation. However, several factors decrease the likelihood of it occurring anytime soon. First of all, a reproducing population obviously requires a male and female cat. While young females have journeyed away from the Black Hills, most of the dispersers are young males. At the present time the prospects of two dispersers meeting and mating in suitable habitat to the east are quite small. Perhaps more important, many states in which mountain lions might become established east of their current range have minimal or no legal protection for the animals. A considerable number of dispersers have been shot in states where both cougars and legal protection for them are absent. Along those lines, the dispersing cats would most likely move through eastern North Dakota and South Dakota. In neither state are mountain lions sufficiently protected outside their current range to ensure wandering adolescents could make the eastern journey in large enough numbers to up the odds of males and females crossing paths in viable habitat. While many wildlife advocates would like to see mountain lions established in habitats to the east of their range, current conditions make the odds of a natural recolonization very small.

The tracks of wandering cougars are occasionally found east of their current range. Establishing populations will take more legal protection and toleration of mountain lions by human residents. NPS Photo

but mountain lions may also rely on other types of prey, including bighorn sheep, wild pigs, porcupines, various types of rabbits and hares, and a host of other small mammals and birds. Mountain lions sometimes thrive in harsh environments that hold good numbers of potential prey species. They are currently abundant in many areas classified as desert in the American Southwest. Wilderness areas in central Idaho are often characterized by steep terrain and cold winters with deep snow, yet mountain lion populations remain healthy in these daunting environments as well.

Along with a reliable prey base, mountain lions need habitat that supports their hunting techniques and buffers them from competitive predators. Cougars are often described as a "spot and ambush" predator, meaning they habitually sneak close to a potential prey animal, then rush in to catch it from a close distance. This is easiest to accomplish where forest cover, shrubbery, desert scrub, and geological features such as rocks, cliffs, and gullies provide mountain lions with ideal places in which to approach and ambush prey undetected. They also use trees and cliffs to elude competitive predators, which include grizzly and black bears, wolves, and coyotes. Mountain lions are at a serious

Mountain lions may use cliffs and stone outcroppings for stalking prey, but these features may also help them avoid other predators. This cougar is traversing a rock face in Lake Mead National Recreation Area in Nevada. NPS Photo

disadvantage on flat expanses of unbroken prairie, both from the standpoint of successfully ambushing prey and keeping themselves and their kills safe from other predators.

Human disturbance is another factor that currently dictates mountain lion habitat. Areas used extensively for agriculture, especially large expanses of cleared croplands, are unsuitable to mountain lions. Some of the enterprising cats have taken up residence in suburban areas, but they are often lethally removed as a potential threat to people, pets, and livestock. Additionally, mortality from vehicle collisions claims many cougars each year. Even if a semi-urban area contains a robust population of whitetail deer (a favorite prey of many mountain lions), if it is riddled with roads, mountain lions may not survive.

The best home for a mountain lion occurs where large expanses of native habitat remain intact. In such locations, cougars play a valuable role in balancing the populations of their prey species and creating a healthier ecosystem for other animals.

Chapter 3 Abilities and Behavior

Physical Abilities

An ambush predator such as the cougar must rely on stealth and skillful use of cover to get close to its prey. Once within range, the cat's success is highly dependent on the speed of its attack. What adaptations allow the mountain lion to successfully hunt deer and other ungulates that can run 30 miles per hour or faster?

Mountain lions have very long, muscular hind legs, proportionately longer than those of other members of the cat family. Their spine is also long and flexible, similar to that of the cheetah. Muscles along the spine, as well as those found on the legs, are used to propel the mountain lion's body in a chase. These physical characteristics facilitate some of the cougar's most amazing

Mountain lions can cover up to 40 feet in a single bound. Licensed by Shutterstock.com

Mountain lions are very fast but tire quickly due to limited lung capacity. LICENSED BY SHUTTERSTOCK.COM

athletic abilities. Estimates vary, but it is commonly reported that mountain lions can sprint from 40 to 50 miles per hour over short distances. The exceptional length and strength of their hind legs, coupled with a spine that allows the hind feet to reach far under the body for leverage in making a bound, give the cats a remarkable ability to accelerate in as few as two leaps. Mountain lions may cover as much as 40 feet in a single bound. It is often reported that they can clear up to 15 feet in a single vertical leap.

However, when compared to most of their prey and other predators such as wolves that often use long-distance chases to tire their victims, mountain lions have a notably limited lung capacity. This diminishes the distance over which they can effectively pursue prey, and also makes them susceptible to attacks from rival predators with more stamina if caught in the open. Thus, when chased by other dangerous animals, such as wolves or a pack of hunting dogs, mountain lions typically climb a tree or flee to other cover where the pursuers are unable to follow, such as elevated rock ledges or stony spires. Mountain lions seem very aware of the limits of their endurance in relation to their prey. If a fleet of foot prey animal such as a whitetail deer is not caught within a short distance, an adult cougar will very quickly abandon the chase.

The large paws of a mountain lion are outfitted with large, very sharp retractable claws. The mountain lion's flexible, expansive paws and soft, furry underbelly allow it to crawl almost silently across nearly any terrain in approach of prey. Five claws are found in each of the front feet, one of which is associated with the dewclaw (thumb). The dewclaw and its claw do not bear any weight and are not used in running. They are very instrumental, however, in the lion's ability to grasp and hold prey. Each rear paw has four claws, which may be used in subduing prey and in self-defense, though their function is certainly secondary to the claws on the forepaws. Mountain lions are very adept at climbing trees. The sharp, curved claws on their hind feet allow them to propel themselves quickly up a tree trunk, while the claws on the front feet are used to grasp bark and branches. Like ordinary house cats, mountain lions are very comfortable in moving about in trees, an ability directly related to the shape and strength of their claws.

The mountain lion's retractable claws are one of the features that help naturalists distinguish the cats' paw prints from those of canines, including coyotes, foxes, and wolves. Any track that shows claw marks along with pad prints do not belong to a mountain lion (or any other member of the cat family in North America). Claw marks left by a coyote's foot may be hard to pick out on bare ground or in vegetation. In snow, mud, or soft ground, they are usually quite evident and serve as one of the distinguishing features separating canine tracks from cougar prints.

Their oversize paws also help make mountain lions capable swimmers. Contrary to some portrayals, cougars are very comfortable around water and cross sizeable bodies of water with ease.

Mountain lions, like this one photographed in Grand Teton National Park, are good swimmers and at ease around water. NPS PHOTO

Incredible sprinting speed and sharp claws enable mountain lions to catch and hold their prey. Specialized teeth, bones, and jaw muscles are the lethal weapons the cats then use to kill those animals. Compared to many other predators, mountain lions have fewer teeth. The mouth of an adult cougar contains just thirty teeth, while dogs, foxes, and other North American canines have forty-two, as do black, polar, and grizzly bears. The bite of a raccoon includes forty teeth, while wolverines have thirty-eight teeth.

Having fewer teeth is not a disadvantage to a mountain lion's killing methods. It means greater force is exerted on each tooth. The cougar's four canine teeth (fangs) are stout and long and do not bend in any direction. They are responsible for the penetrating wounds usually directed at the back of the neck or throat of the cat's prey. Smaller animals are often killed with a single bite to the back of the neck, where the fangs slide between the vertebrae

27

Strong specialized teeth allow mountain lions to kill much of their prey with a single bite to the back of the neck. Licensed by Shutterstock.com

to cut the spinal cord. Behind the canine teeth are premolars and molars, comparatively longer and sharper than those of bears and canines. These allow mountain lions to easily slice through flesh and may aid them in delivering a suffocating bite to the throat of their prey. However, these teeth are not as efficient for crushing and chewing. Unlike bears and wolves, which often crack surprisingly large bones to eat the marrow, mountain lions' teeth are not adapted for chewing or crushing bones.

The muscles that close a mountain lion's jaws are highly developed and attached to the lower jaw in a manner promoting leverage, which results in very powerful bite force. Such strong muscles and large teeth exert massive force on the jaw. Both the upper and lower jaws have reinforcement-like portions of bone, rendering the jaws highly resistant to bending or breaking.

Mountain lions commonly hunt and travel at night or in the low-light hours of dawn and dusk. Their eyes are equipped with oversize pupils that allow abundant light to reach the retina on the rear side of the eyeball. The retina contains a preponderance of rod cells, which facilitate vision in low light. A layer of reflective tissue common to nocturnal (active at night) animals, called the *tapetum lucidum*, enhances light transmission within a mountain lion's eyes. It is this tissue that also causes the cat's eyes (and those of other nocturnal animals) to glow when struck by headlights or other bright light sources. In addition to having superior light-gathering properties in the dark, the mountain lion's eyes also have corneas (the clear front windows of the eyes) that provide a very broad field of binocular vision and acute depth perception. These sensory abilities are thought to assist the cat in delivering precise bites and blows to its prey. The cougar's daylight vision is at least as good as that of a human. Biologists theorize the cat's night vision is six times better than that of people. This is based on the fact that mountain lions require just 17 percent as much light to detect details in the visual world as humans do at night. The long whiskers on a cougar's nose also help it to avoid obstacles in night navigation and are thought by some biologists to guide the cat's teeth when biting prey.

The mountain lion's vision is probably the sense most responsible for its hunting skill. However, the animals also rely on a keen sense of hearing equal to or better than that of humans to detect prey, sense danger, and communicate with members of their own kind. In fact, mountain lions are capable of hearing high-frequency sounds undetectable to the human ear.

The role of smell as a hunting tool for mountain lions is poorly understood. Some research indicates the olfactory (smelling) sensitivity of a cougar is roughly thirty times greater than that of a human. In comparison to hoofed animals like deer and elk, or other predators such as coyotes and bears, a mountain lion's sense of smell is quite weak. (Scientists estimate wolves and grizzly bears have a sense of smell that is perhaps one thousand times more sensitive than a human's.) Nonetheless, observational studies of hunting mountain lions support the notion that they do use their noses when hunting. Researchers have documented mountain lions approaching bedded prey animals that the cat likely did not locate by sight. Mountain lions most often approach their prey from downwind, a tactic necessary to keep their own scent from drifting to their potential victim, but a method perhaps also favored by their ability to smell their prey.

Vocal and Visual Communication

Humans rarely observe the lives of wild mountain lions. Some evidence of their vocalizations is available, but exactly how and why mountain lions make sounds under natural conditions is not clearly understood.

The most dramatic noise uttered by the cougar is its scream, a call some researchers describe as the "caterwaul." This call is likened to the mating call a domestic female cat produces when she is ready to mate, and it probably serves the same purpose. In comparison to a housecat's cry, the caterwaul of a mountain lion is very loud and high-pitched, often described as the sound of a woman screaming in distress. Researchers believe this call is normally issued by female mountain lions to attract males when they are ready to mate. While the high-pitched screaming aspect of the caterwaul is most readily heard from a distance, the call may also contain lower-pitched and less voluminous pieces, including purring and mewing.

Other sounds mountain lions emit are also similar to those heard from domestic cats. Very young cougars (under two weeks old) emit a bleating or sharp, high-pitched mewing sound indicating distress. Both mother and young mountain lions purr as a sound of contentment, and a female cougar may purr as a means of communicating assurance to her entire litter.

Spitting, hissing, and growling are common ways housecats indicate their displeasure. Mountain lions make equivalent vocalizations for similar purposes. Numerous researchers have been confronted by hissing and growling as they approached a mountain lion confined in a cage-trap or snare. Hunters using dogs to "tree" mountain lions also report hearing these "do not approach" type of sounds.

Mountain lions make a variety of sounds including growling and hissing. Licensed by
SHUTTERSTOCK.COM

A vocalization occasionally used by both male and female mountain lions is sometimes dubbed the "ouch" call, for its similarity to the iconic noise uttered by a human who drops a cup on his bare toes. Its purpose isn't clearly understood. Some researchers have witnessed it as perhaps a vocal indication of frustration after an unsuccessful predation attempt. Others believe it may be used to announce a mountain lion's presence to others.

A yowling call is common to both genders of adult mountain lions. It is thought other cats may be able to discern the sex, age, and stature of the yowler. This call may help cougars avoid surprise encounters with other animals, or perhaps it aids in the maintenance of a territory.

Social Structure and Dynamics

Mountain lions are notoriously solitary creatures. They rarely hunt cooperatively as African lions do. The exception to this rule may be a female in the company of her sub-adult young. In fact, females with young are the only group of mountain lions known to regularly exist together as a social unit.

Both male and female mountain lions utilize home ranges, expanses of habitat that might be seen as an animal's neighborhood from which it rarely strays. Male cougars also claim territories, specific geographical areas that they defend against other males. Researchers have documented some overlap in the ranges of both sexes, with females showing a tolerance for other females within their home range. Studies have indicated that the home ranges of female mountain lions sometimes overlap by over 50 percent. However, within the home range most females occupy a core area that is less regularly encroached upon by other females. While male territories often overlap on the fringes, studies conducted with radio collars indicate adult male mountain lions seldom deliberately penetrate the core of another male's territory, typically with hostile intent.

Homes ranges among female mountain lions in North America have been documented to cover as little as 21 square miles and as much as 300 square miles. Research indicates that females

Female cougars caring for young may temporarily reduce their home range to provide security for their offspring. Licensed by Shutterstock.com

sometimes occupy two seasonal home ranges where their primary prey base (such as mule deer) is migratory. Deer and other ungulates frequently move from summer to winter range, necessitating a shift in a mountain lion's range as well. The range of female mountain lions shrinks considerably when they are raising young, particularly in the first two months after birth.

Adult male cougars are aggressively territorial. On average the territories of male cougars are considerably larger than those of females. Normally the range of a single male mountain lion will overlap those of several females. Their territories are usually 50 percent to 300 percent larger than those of adult females. Researchers have discovered male mountain lion territories in North America ranging from 58 square miles to more than 300 square miles. Despite some overlap in territories, males monitored by researchers have shown an uncanny ability to avoid areas of overlap currently occupied by a rival.

Male cougars make scrapes within their territories, often on ridges or other well-frequented travel routes. Scrapes are created when the males scratch the ground with their hind legs. Unlike some other species of cats that leave scent on a scrape via urination, male cougars' create their scrapes by scratching alone. Biologists theorize the scrapes are used as territorial markings to announce the presence of the local tom to others. Evidence of this theory is found in the fact that researchers have seldom documented scrapes made by females or immature adults.

Large, combative male mountain lions are the most successful at claiming a territory and producing offspring. Oftentimes they are also the number one reason other cougars die in nonhunted populations. Adult male mountain lions are known to aggressively kill cubs sired by another male. Many biologists believe death at the fangs of an adult male is the leading cause of mortality to young cougars. Eliminating the offspring of another male accomplishes two purposes. First, it rids the population of rival genes to the dominating male. More important, perhaps, females who are not caring for cubs become reproductively active. By killing a female's kittens, a male may incite her to mate.

Males also kill females, especially if the two have not been engaged in a previous breeding relationship. Adult males often kill females that are attempting to defend their young. They may also fatally attack a female to claim the carcass of killed prey. Some researchers have recorded instances where female mountain lions have been killed and eaten by males for food.

Battles between male mountain lions are usually fierce and unforgiving. In the absence of human-caused mortality, such as hunting or vehicle collisions, fatal interactions between male cougars are the primary source of survival risk. Both female and male cougars tend to disperse (move to a different territory than the one used by their mother) as they reach adulthood. Males tend to disperse farther than females. Dispersing males must either claim a territory uninhabited by another male or fight with an established tom to conquer its range. Dominant males may also fight to

Interactions between mountain lions, especially those involving adult males, are often violent. Strife between cougars is a significant source of mortality in most populations.

EPIC DISPERSALS, EXTREME DANGERS

As they achieve independence from their mother, most young mountain lions move to new territory. This phenomenon is known as a "dispersal" in the world of cougar research. Most mountain lions are around eighteen to twenty-four months of age when they disperse.

Research indicates males generally travel farther when dispersing than females, but young females sometimes migrate substantial distances. For example, one young radio-collared female traveled from north-central Utah to northwestern Colorado, where she was shot by a hunter. At the time of death, she was 221 miles from the site of her capture, but her collar documented her journey covered 833 miles in one year and one day.

Young males have dispersed from occupied habitat in the West to as far-flung locations as Missouri. DNA analysis of tissue or hair collected from three mountain lions killed or sighted in Missouri in 2011 indicated dispersals from central Montana, Colorado, and South Dakota. The most famous dispersal of a mountain lion came to an end on June 11, 2011, when a three-year-old male was struck and killed by a car in Milford, Connecticut. The cat was born in the Black Hills of South Dakota and had dispersed some 1,500 miles from his birthplace in a journey that probably covered over 2,000 miles.

While such dramatic dispersals underscore the fascinating nature of mountain lions, they almost invariably come to a tragic end. Most are terminated when young cats enter states without legal protection and are shot, or they are killed by vehicles and sometimes trains. Young cats disperse in an effort to find a mate and new territory in suitable habitat. In the absence of either, they continue to wander, lowering their odds of survival as they go.

enlarge their territory or when they encounter one another where their geographical spheres of influence overlap.

Interactions between toms in any of the above scenarios frequently leads to the death of one of the males. Depending on the severity of the wounds sustained by the victor, it is possible that both males may eventually die as a result of the battle. A study of mountain lions in New Mexico recorded thirty-five interactions between male cougars. Nearly 30 percent of those encounters resulted in the death of one of the males. A few of the fatalities occurred at carcasses, but most of them involved males vying for territory or directly competing for breeding rights to a female.

The mountain lion's social web is characterized by a generally solitary life and extreme strife and violence instigated by males. However, a handful of recent observations by researchers indicate that rarely encountered social dynamics exist and paint a somewhat different picture of cougar interactions. For example, researchers in the Jackson, Wyoming, area (home to Grand Teton National Park) have documented amicable social interactions between adult mountain lions, including two unrelated females with kittens that often shared kills. Within the mostly solitary, often violent world of mountain lions, there appears to be a range of more peaceful and perhaps cooperative behaviors biologists have yet to observe and understand.

Chapter 4 Mountain Lions and Other Animals

Mountain Lions and Their Prey: Prey Species

The mountain lion's diet consists almost entirely of other animals that it obtains through predation and occasionally by scavenging or stealing a kill from a less formidable predator. Mountain lions normally focus on prey species that weigh 50 percent as much as they do or larger. The efficiency of cougars in killing large prey is extraordinary. Of all the large cats in the world, mountain lions bring down the largest prey in relation to their own size. It is not uncommon for mountain lions to prey upon animals whose weight is more than twice their own.

However, mountain lions are known to dine on smaller animals as well. The extent to which they utilize smaller prey is somewhat unclear. Biologists who study mountain lions most often rely on tracking data from radio collars to ascertain a cougar has made a kill. The site is then investigated, and data—including the species, gender, approximate age, and weight of the prey—are recorded. However, a cougar nabbing a cottontail rabbit while on the move won't register on a radio collar (researchers often know a cat has made a larger kill when it remains in one place for a period of time). Furthermore, the carcasses of smaller creatures may be completely consumed by a mountain lion, leaving nothing behind for a biologist to analyze. Remains of rodents, birds, and other little creatures may show up in mountain lion scat. The presence of a prey item in scat, however, doesn't provide definitive information about the extent to which it occurs in the cougar's diet and its significance to its overall nutrition.

What types of animals will mountain lions target for prey? Researchers have recorded them consuming reptiles, birds (such as ruffed grouse and wild turkeys), and mammals. Amphibians, fish, and other aquatic creatures may be eaten as well, although the frequency with which this happens is unclear. In South America some cougars consume iguanas and caiman (an alligator-like reptile) on a somewhat regular basis and are also known to prey upon bats. A general rule appears to govern mountain lion predation in relation to latitude: Those in tropical and subtropical regions rely on smaller prey to a greater extent than those in northern regions.

Ground squirrels and marmots are among the smaller prey sometimes taken by mountain lions. The cats are also known to kill opossums and moles. Rabbits and hares are another source of pint-size prey and may be a very important food source in some habitats, especially when the bunnies are at the peak of their population cycle. Research projects in Utah, Washington, and Florida indicate rabbits and hares may represent over 10 percent of some cougar's annual diet.

Armadillos are among some of the unusual prey species frequently eaten by mountain lions. Licensed by Shutterstock.com

Slightly larger prey taken by mountain lions include beavers and porcupines. In fact, some mountain lions become very adept at killing porcupines. Where they are abundant in the Rocky Mountains, porcupines comprise up to 20 percent of a mountain lion's annual diet, according to some studies. Collared peccary (javelina), a type of pig-like animal found in the southwestern United States, are an important prey species to some mountain lions. Weighing from thirty-five to sixty pounds, an adult peccary represents a substantial meal, especially to a sub-adult or small female cougar. Mountain lions also prey upon armadillos. Some studies indicate armadillos make up 10 percent or more of the diet of some Florida panthers.

Mountain lions also have a taste for feral hogs. Domestic pigs turned wild have become a significant problem in many parts of the country due to their damage of crops and wildlife habitat. Some cougars regularly prey upon feral hogs in Texas and California. One study of Florida panthers indicated that feral hogs may comprise up to 59 percent of the annual diet of some cats. Mountain lions in some places in the Southwest also prey upon feral horses. In both cases the native cats are eliminating potentially destructive nonnative species (neither domestic hogs nor horses are native to North America) from native ecosystems.

However, in most habitats in North America, ungulate prey species of the deer family compose the "lion's share" of a cougar's diet. Evolutionary biologists theorize that the mountain lion's solitary and specialized hunting strategies are most efficient when targeted at the largest animals they can reasonably subdue. For example, stalking and rushing a 250-pound mule deer may require the same amount of time and skill as sneaking up on and snatching a 4-pound rabbit. Although the deer may represent more risk of bodily harm to the predator, it also enables the cat to feed for several days, providing enough energy for the mountain lion to turn its attention to other critical biological tasks such as defending a territory, searching for mates, or rearing young.

The types of ungulates mountain lions routinely prey upon differ by geographic region and abundance, but in most places,

Mule and whitetail deer, along with elk, are the major prey animals for mountain lions over most of their range in the United States.

mule and whitetail deer make up the bulk of the typical cougar's diet, especially in winter. Numerous research projects throughout the northern and southern Rocky Mountains have found deer represent 85 percent or more of mountain lions' diet in places where they are abundant. However, the cat regularly preys upon other ungulates as well. In one study in British Columbia, researchers recorded elk comprising as high as 69 percent of the annual predation of a sample of mountain lions. Prior to the reintroduction of wolves into Yellowstone National Park, researchers found that elk were the number one source of prey for mountain lions in the northern part of the park, which held an exceptionally large elk population. Mountain lions also kill moose with some frequency in Alberta, British Columbia, and Idaho. Adult elk and moose are infrequently targeted by mountain lions, unless they are weakened. Immature animals of both species are those most routinely killed by cougars.

Bighorn sheep are also a mountain lion's preferred prey in some local areas; so much so that reintroduction of bighorns in some places in the southwestern United States has been hampered by cougar predation. Mountain lions are also known to feed on pronghorn (antelope) and mountain goats, although these animals typically inhabit terrain in which the hunting skills of cougars are not usually effective.

Studies of mountain lion predation on ungulates reveal some interesting tendencies. As might be expected, larger mountain lions tend to target larger prey. A robust male cougar weighing 150 pounds is far more likely than a 90-pound female to make a predation attempt on an adult elk. One study in Alberta reported that nearly 70 percent of the kills made by male cougars were moose, mostly calves. By contrast, moose represented less than 5 percent of the kills made by female mountain lions. Regardless of gender, some mountain lions appear to specialize in taking certain prey species more frequently than others. Several studies have documented specific lions downing an unusually high percentage of the bighorn sheep preyed upon by the big cats in local areas. For example, one team of researchers studying mountain lions in New Mexico recorded four bighorn sheep kills by mountain lions. Of those, three were made by the same male cougar.

Mountain lions also have the ability to readily switch between prey sources, depending on abundance or scarcity. As mentioned previously, hares and rabbits are regularly targeted in seasons of abundance. One study in Idaho found mountain lions dining heavily on ground squirrels in the summer, when they are plenteous. Researchers in British Columbia found snowshoe hares made up around 25 percent of the mountain lions' diet during the peak of the bunnies' reproductive cycle. Following a crash in the mule deer population in Big Bend National Park in Texas, biologists observed cougars switching from deer to rabbits, hares, and collared peccaries as their primary sources of prey.

Mountain Lions and Their Prey: Hunting Strategies

Mountain lions and wolves commonly prey upon many of the same species of animals where their range overlaps, yet their predation strategies are very different. Whereas wolves often test the fitness of a single animal or animals within a herd through an extended chase or harassment, cougars appear to make up their minds about attacking an animal in advance. Wolves often chase their prey for long distances before bringing it down. Mountain lions abandon the chase very quickly if unsuccessful. Wolves thus belong to the family of coursing (chasing) predators, while cougars are aligned with other meat eaters who stalk their prey.

As mentioned in chapter 3, mountain lions can run very fast, but they sustain their blinding speeds only over short distances. Thus, they attempt to get very close to their prey before rushing to seize it. One study concluded that mountain lions were most successful when they stalked within less than 10 feet of mule deer and contacted the targeted animal within less than 35 feet.

Cover plays an important role in the mountain lion's hunting techniques. Their hunting is most successful where ground cover (rocks, trees, brush, and so on) is heavy enough to aid in their concealment as they approach their prey, but open enough to allow a fairly unobstructed field of vision. Mountain lions are very adept

Cover is essential for mountain lions to approach prey closely enough for a successful ambush. Licensed by Shutterstock.com

at advancing slowly on their bellies, their soft fur and padded feet allowing them to move nearly soundlessly. Like housecats, their ability to remain motionless for long periods of time is remarkable. Similar to domestic cats, the tip of a mountain lion's tail might twitch slightly in anticipation as it closes the distance on potential prey.

Much is made of wolves' ability to detect and exploit weakness among ungulates. Packs frequently kill older animals or those weakened by disease or injury. The canines are evidently able to perceive vulnerabilities as they harass or chase elk and deer, motivating them to sustain the attack until successful.

Research involving mountain lion predation reveals a nearly identical pattern. Ungulates killed by mountain lions are typically older or weaker than their counterparts. In the case of a bull elk blinded in one eye and weakened by an antler wound to its head from fighting a rival during mating season, a mountain lion can obviously perceive vulnerability that would also be obvious to a human. But older animals do not often appear weak or out of shape to a person's eye. Yet mountain lions have an uncanny ability to mark them for predation. They evidently sense other weakness as well. Chronic wasting disease (CWD) is a malady often affecting mule and whitetail deer in various regions of the country. Prior to its final stages, animals infected with CWD show no visible signs of the infection. However, one study in a mule deer population where CWD was present discovered that mountain lions preyed upon infected animals four times more often than those that were uninfected. Some biologists believe mountain lions have a remarkably sophisticated ability to observe very subtle aspects of behavior and appearance in their prey that indicate greater vulnerability to a predatory attack.

After stealthily closing the distance to their prey, mountain lions bound swiftly to catch the animal, normally contacting it within a few leaps. The cats use their curved, exceedingly sharp claws to grasp and control the fleeing animal. Smaller prey is normally killed with a fatal bite directed to the neck, just behind the skull, or a bite to the back of the skull that pierces to the brain. Larger prey, such as deer-size animals, may be dispatched with a bite to the neck. However, mountain lions often kill creatures larger than themselves by directing their fangs to the animal's throat, crushing its airway and strangling it. Larger animals killed by mountain lions often have extensive claw marks on the nose and cheeks. Mountain lions use their powerful forelegs and claws to cling to struggling prey. Sometimes cougars kill ungulate prey swiftly, at other times the struggle may span several minutes and cover considerable distance, occasionally up to 100 yards.

Once a kill has been made, mountain lions normally drag their prey to a sheltered location to feed. This behavior evidently decreases the odds of the cat losing its meal to a wolf pack, bear, or other rival predators. Some biologists also theorize cougars transport prey to more secretive locations to avoid the attention of scavenging birds such as ravens and magpies, which might more easily attract the attention of a larger scavenger like a grizzly bear.

A deer-size ungulate will normally keep a cougar at the carcass for twelve hours to three days, sometimes up to a week. After the kill, most mountain lions feed heavily on the carcass, first consuming the heart, liver, lungs, and diaphragm. These organs are easily obtained once the body cavity is torn open, and they are highly nutritious. The cats then turn their attention to other digestive organs and fats. Afterward they consume muscle tissues, but they do not attempt to eat or gnaw on bones. Between feeding sessions, mountain lions "cache" the carcass, covering it with sticks, grass, or soil. Some research indicates male cougars may consume from twenty to thirty pounds of flesh from a carcass in the initial feeding.

The extent to which a mountain lion fully consumes a prey animal depends on the size of the prey and the cougar. Smaller prey are normally eaten in full. Larger prey are often consumed relative to the cat's size and gender. On average, big toms eat the smallest percentage of a carcass, lightweight females consume the highest percentage. This is likely due to the disparity of effort in making a kill between the two classes of cougars. A large male has an easier time bringing down a deer than a small female and thus has the luxury of dining on only the choice parts of the carcass, or so many biologists assume.

As noted previously, mountain lions often attack prey more than twice as large as themselves. Ungulate prey are equipped with hard, sharp hooves. Depending on the time of the year, male ungulates may also sport dangerous antlers. Cougars are amazingly effective predators, but their carnivorous lifestyle comes with many risks. In rare instances mountain lions may be directly killed in a predation attempt. For example, researchers in Yellowstone National Park once found the body of a bighorn ram and a mountain lion that had tried to kill it at the base of a cliff from which both animals had fallen. The robust five-year-old male cougar died from the impact of the fall. Injuries sustained in predation attempts can prove indirectly fatal, too. Mountain lions gored by an antler tip may later succumb to infection. Dislocated joints or other injuries sustained in predation may render the cat unable to hunt, leading to starvation.

Mountain Lions and Other Predators

The number of prey species that are themselves predators recorded in the diets of mountain lions is astonishing. Raccoons are commonly killed and consumed by Florida panthers. Ringtails and coatis, relatives of the raccoon that live in the desert Southwest, are also sometimes eaten by mountain lions. Mountain lions often dine upon skunks, with some evidence indicating that some sub-adult cougars perhaps specialize in killing skunks as they mature. Incidences of mountain lions in North America eating weasels, gray foxes, badgers, bobcats, coyotes, wolves, otters, and black

Young mountain lions are at risk from other predators. This young cougar was trapped on a fence on the National Elk Refuge in Jackson Hole, Wyoming, by a pack of aggressive coyotes. USFWS Photo–Lori Iverson

bears have also been recorded. As noted in chapter 3, mountain lions may also kill and eat other mountain lions. In the case of the previously mentioned predators, they are sometimes eaten after being killed by a mountain lion, sometimes not. Whether a cougar eats another predator it has dispatched is possibly determined by how hungry the cat is at the time. How can a mountain lion stand to eat something as foul-smelling (and tasting) as a skunk or weasel? Mountain lions have far fewer taste buds than humans and many other creatures. Perhaps this is why they sometimes gladly chow down on a stinky skunk.

Mountain lions have been documented killing coyotes, wolves, and bears. However, these creatures also infrequently end the lives of mountain lions. Kittens and sub-adults are at the greatest danger from coyotes, although packs of coyotes can capably drive some adult mountain lions from their kill. On the other hand, an adult lion can handily chase a coyote from a carcass. Coyotes and similar-size predators are typically killed by a mountain lion with a crushing bite to the back of the skull or the neck.

The interactions among mountain lions, wolves, and bears are oftentimes complex. Under the right circumstances, each of these creatures can be a lethal threat to one another, although cougars are typically at a disadvantage due to the superior size of a mature black or grizzly bear and the overwhelming numbers of a wolf pack. However, mountain lions are not always on the losing side of the confrontations. Researchers in the Jackson, Wyoming, area documented a female mountain lion killing and eating a young wolf that was apparently part of a pack. Canadian researchers have also found evidence of cougars lethally interacting with single wolves.

In most situations, however, a wolf pack is a much greater threat to a mountain lion than the converse. Studies in Yellowstone National Park and Banff National Park (Canada) concluded wolves usurped (stole by force) between 6 percent and 14 percent of cougar kills in the study areas. Research in the parks and other areas, including central Idaho and Glacier National Park in

Recent research suggests grizzly bears frequently steal kills from mountain lions where they share range. Where prevalent, this practice may negatively affect cougar numbers.

northwestern Montana, indicated wolves visited mountain lion kill sites quite frequently (up to 33 percent), although the extent to which wolves drove the cat from the carcass is unknown.

Grizzly bears commonly usurp carcasses from cougars. The keen nose of the grizzly bear is exceptionally suited for smelling and can likely detect the scent of a freshly killed carcass from over a mile away. One study of grizzly bears in Yellowstone and Glacier National Parks found the bears displaced mountain lions from 50 percent (Glacier) and 37 percent (Yellowstone) of the observed carcasses. Other research in the Glacier National Park area has indicated routine usurpation of mountain lion prey by grizzly bears and wolves may exert considerable stress on cougars, perhaps leading to malnutrition or, in extreme cases, starvation. Taking down an elk or deer is an energy intensive, physically

PRICKLY PREY

Fishers are one of the few predators routinely successful in preying upon porcupines. A member of the weasel family, fishers normally weigh from five to twelve pounds, smaller than the average porcupine. Fishers kill porcupines with swift, repeated bites to the head in a sustained predation attack that takes twenty minutes or more.

Mountain lions also feed upon porcupines, occasionally in extremely high numbers. Biologists have documented a young male mountain lion killing thirty-five porcupines in the span of three months in Colorado. A young female in Wyoming took twenty-four in two and a half months. Cougar predation on porcupines may substantially impact local numbers. A small population of porcupines in Nevada was reduced by over 90 percent in three years due to mountain lion predation.

However, preying upon porcupines isn't without risk. It is not clearly known how mountain lions kill porcupines, although evidence indicates at least some cats learn to harass them into falling from trees, where they are killed or sustain debilitating injuries on contact with the ground. Some folklore claims cougars reach a paw under the porcupine's quill-less belly and flip it over, though there is no biological evidence of which I am aware to support this theory. Regardless of the method, mountain lions are

dangerous task for a mountain lion. If the cat loses its bounty to a competing predator, it must soon kill again. It appears that this equation can become very costly to mountain lions, especially in habitats where they must contend with both wolves and grizzly bears.

sometimes impaled with quills when preying upon porcupines. The results can be fatal.

The sharp quills of porcupines have a barb on the end. When driven into the muscle of an attacker, the quill works itself deeper into the flesh as the muscle expands and contracts. Heat from the attacker's body enlarges the barb, making it even more tenacious. Interestingly, quills do not carry infection. These specialized hairs are covered with a peculiar compound possessed of antibacterial characteristics, evidently an adaptation that protects porcupines from infection when they're accidentally stuck with their own quills.

Over time quills may migrate from the skin and outer tissues of an impaled aggressor into the body cavity, puncturing vital organs or causing wounds susceptible to infection. Young mountain lions learning to hunt apparently kill porcupines by leaping upon them, at least in some cases. Researchers have recorded multiple instances in which mountain lions have been killed by porcupines. In one well-documented case in Wyoming, an autopsy of the dead young female showed one lung completely destroyed by the aftermath of a quill invasion, the other severely lacerated. Mountain lions are among a very tiny handful of North American predators fearless enough to prey on porcupines. Sometimes the porcupine wins in the end.

Parasites and Diseases

Mountain lions are often described as being largely free of parasites and diseases, although such a conclusion may be in error due to the very limited research that has been conducted on these conditions in wild cougars. The cats sometimes harbor intestinal parasites such as roundworms and tapeworms. Mountain lions sometimes deliberately consume grass, a behavior some biologists believe may aid in expelling such parasites. External parasite such as ticks, fleas, and mites may also infest cougars.

Documented deaths of mountain lions due to disease are rare. On just two occasions have cougars been confirmed dying from rabies: one of those cases occurred in 1909, the other more recently in Florida. A California mountain lion was diagnosed with feline leukemia and was euthanized (killed to prevent suffering). One expert familiar with the case believed the cougar contacted the disease from preying upon domestic cats.

At the present time it is believed that parasites and diseases are not a significant factor in mountain lion mortality or health. As the lives of these elusive cats become more thoroughly understood through research, a more precise understanding of the role of these maladies may alter current perceptions.

Chapter 5 Reproduction and Young

The Mating Season

In contrast to animals with a defined mating and birthing season (wolf pups in the wild, for example, are always born in the spring), mountain lions may mate during any season of the year. However, in North America most cougars mate from late fall to early spring. Mountain lions are polygamous, meaning one male may mate with multiple females, and a single female may mate with several toms.

When a female enters estrus and is prepared to mate, she seeks scrapes made by male cougars and calls to announce her presence and readiness to breed. The advertising female may attract the attention of more than one male, resulting in heated combat between the males.

Courtship rituals between wild mountain lions are rarely observed by humans. However, it is known that mating usually occurs over a period of several days in which the pair may mate as many as fifty times per day. After mating with one male, a female may mate with another. Mating appears to develop peaceful relationships between male and female cougars. Females are less likely to be attacked by males with which they have mated, giving themselves and their offspring a higher chance of survival when encountering a male.

Mating is one of the few times during the year when relationships are peaceful between male and female mountain lions.
Licensed by Shutterstock.com

53

Pregnancy and Gestation

Because female mountain lions sometimes mate with more than one male, it is possible that kittens in the same litter may have different fathers. This phenomenon has been observed in other polygamous species, but the extent to which it occurs in mountain lion populations is unknown. The gestation period (the time from mating to birth) for mountain lions averages around ninety-two days. Thus the female give birth three months after becoming pregnant.

Birth

Female mountain lions give birth to their young in a den of sorts, typically a protected space under a rock ledge, between overlapping boulders, or in a patch of very dense vegetation providing cover from the sides and overhead. Unlike the den sites of wolves and coyotes that often enlarge or modify a hole through digging, female mountain lions are not known to alter natural den sites. Many biologists thus prefer to call the site in which a mountain births and cares for her young in the first weeks of life a *nursery* as opposed to a *den*. If the nursery is threatened before the young are ready to leave, the mother may move them to an alternate rearing site, carrying each kitten carefully in her mouth.

Baby cougars are tiny, with average birth weights scarcely exceeding one pound (around eighteen ounces). Mountain lion kittens are quite helpless at birth. They are covered in fur at birth with coats ranging from reddish brown to grayish brown. Black spots adorn their coats, black rings are found on their tails. Stripes, or a series of continuous spots that nearly form a stripe, sometimes run along the kitten's back. The eyes and ears of newborn mountain lions are shut. Newborn mountain lions instinctively suckle and nurse soon after birth.

Mountain lion females normally give birth to multiple offspring, but single births can also occur. Litter sizes range from one to six kittens, with three representing the average. At one time biologists speculated younger females birthed fewer kittens on average than older mothers. Recent research, however, indicates

Depressions under overhanging rocks or crevices are used by mountain lions as birthing and nursery sites. Licensed by Shutterstock.com

females birthing their first litter of kittens do not have significantly fewer offspring on average than older females.

Kittens may be born at any time of the year, but in their western range in North America most births (over 70 percent) take place during the seven-month period from May to October. However, within local and regional populations, a "birth pulse" may occur, a biological term used to describe a significant concentration of births within a longer birthing season. Birth pulses among cougars uncannily coincide with prey abundance, which provides mother mountain lions with a readily available food source with which to nourish herself, provide for milk production, and meet the nutritional demands of her litter. Such spikes in mountain lion births typically occur in relation to the birth of ungulate prey, which are normally produced in late May and early June across much of their range in the Rocky Mountains. One study showed mountain lions in Wyoming experienced a birth pulse from August to November, a phenomenon some biologists attribute to the fact that growing kittens and their mothers can take advantage of high numbers of ungulate prey concentrated on winter range about the time the young begin eating larger quantities of meat on their own. Among Florida panthers, a birth pulse occurs from March to July, coinciding with the peak of the fawning period for whitetail deer.

Nurturing Kittens to Adulthood

Within just a few weeks, the helpless kittens change dramatically. Their eyes and ears open by two weeks of age. In contrast to the yellowish eyes of adults, the eyes of baby mountain lions are strikingly blue. By the time they are one month of age, the young have grown mobile and playful, interacting with their siblings through wrestling matches and chasing.

When the kittens are around six to eight weeks of age, the mother cougar leads them from the nursery into a larger and more dangerous world. The cubs follow the female to kill sites, where they learn to feed on the flesh of other animals along with their mother's milk. They have developed quickly. Even at this young age, they are now able to navigate difficult terrain as they accompany their mother. For the next few months their teeth and jaw muscles will develop more fully, allowing them to increasingly ingest larger and less-tender portions of their

The eyes of baby mountain lions are blue. They change to the yellow amber of adult eyes by five months of age. Licensed by Shutterstock.com

By five months of age, mountain lions can easily climb trees, a skill necessary to avoid other predators such as wolves and coyotes. Licensed by Shutterstock.com

mother's prey. This development coincides with a decrease in their mother's milk production. Most cougar kittens are weaned from their mother's milk by three months of age, the timing of which is determined in substantial measure by the nutritional health of the female.

At five months of age, mountain lion kittens have changed dramatically from the tiny, helpless creatures born to their mother. Their eyes have transitioned from baby blue to the amber orbs of adulthood. The black spots on their coats and the dark rings on their tails have faded considerably and will all but disappear by the time they reach their first birthday. Five-month-old cougars can skillfully climb trees, allowing them to flee other antagonistic predators. The kittens have now grown from just over a pound at birth to sixteen to thirty-five pounds, depending on their sex and access to sufficient nutrition.

For the next six to twelve months, young mountain lions will remain with their mother until they achieve independence. During this time they will still be dependent on their mother for food, especially during the first few months. Research indicates female mountain lions with sub-adult kittens around the age of six months are required to kill a mid-size ungulate such as a whitetail deer about every four days. In preparation for independence, the growing cubs must learn to avoid potentially dangerous predators (including adult male cougars) and obtain their own hunting skills, behaviors they will largely acquire from their mother. At one year of age, a young mountain lion has lost its spots, although faint dapples on the coat can often still be detected by researchers or individuals very familiar with cougars. The year-old cougar is approaching its adult weight, although most individuals will continue to grow, sometimes increasing their weight by nearly 50 percent between their first and second birthdays. Occasionally, groups of mountain lions are seen together, perhaps three or four adult-looking cats traveling together in a group. Such sightings sometimes prompt people to report a "pack" or "pride" of mountain lions. In all likelihood these observations include female mountain lions and their nearly grown young. By the time

Sub-adult sibling mountain lions sometimes stay together for a period of time after becoming independent of their mother. Licensed by Shutterstock.com

it reaches the age of independence, a sub-adult male cougar may weigh more than its mother.

Young mountain lions typically separate from their mothers at eleven to eighteen months of age. Their independence is usually triggered by an adult female deliberately abandoning her young, perhaps from a kill site or failing to return to her cubs at a site at which they are resting. Oftentimes the female's separation from her kittens is triggered by her mating or association with a prospective mate. At this point the kittens are on their own, now entering a life stage biologists often describe as the *sub-adult* stage. Newly independent siblings often stay together for a period of time, normally from one to seven weeks, occasionally longer.

The life histories of females and males take different courses during the sub-adult stage. Around half of the females will establish a home range that differs from, but overlaps with, the range of their mother. The other sub-adult females will disperse (travel) away from their mother's home range and take up residence in new territory. Research suggests sub-adult females typically disperse from 10 to 30 miles from their mother's home range. In

A CHALLENGING CHILDHOOD

Mountain lion kittens face a host of hazards in the first six months of life. In some populations, over 50 percent of the kittens born will not likely survive to reach six months of age. Studying the survival rates of mountain lion kittens is difficult. Even in areas undergoing intensive research, it is possible that some young die before investigators discover them.

Of the cubs that fail to survive six months, many are killed by male cougars. In one study in New Mexico, researchers found that 44 percent of the mortalities that occurred in young kittens from birth to 13 months of age, for which a cause was known, were attributed to male mountain lions. Another 37 percent starved to death. Of these, half succumbed to malnutrition because their mother was killed by an adult male. Other kittens starved due to the fact that their mother died in a predation attempt or was taken by illness. Cougar kittens also met their end in accidents (falling from a cliff) and at the jaws of rival predators (coyotes).

contrast, studies have found that all sub-adult male mountain lions disperse from the home range of their mother and migrate much farther than sub-adult females. Studies of cougars in the western United States have shown average dispersal distances of sub-adult males stretching from around 30 to 300 miles.

Sub-adult mountain lions face many challenges. They must sufficiently refine the basic hunting skills learned from their mother to provide for their own nourishment. Traversing unknown territory makes them susceptible to a host of dangers that may include territorial male cougars, human hunters, rival predators, and dangerous roadways. One research project

Young mountain lions face many challenges to reaching adulthood. This sub-adult in Yellowstone Park must dodge wolves, grizzly bears, and many other hazards as it "grows up." NPS PHOTO

Mountain lion kittens are exceedingly cute, engaging creatures. Most are born into treacherous, often violent worlds in which their physical charm provides no assurance of survival.

tracking radio-collared sub-adult cougars discovered male dispersals (the time from which they left their mother's home range to establishing their own territory) spanned from around six to thirty-seven weeks.

If a sub-adult mountain lion lives to establish itself on a home range, it will usually mate and produce young of its own. For both sexes, the age at first reproduction usually occurs between two and three years of age, sometimes a bit sooner.

Chapter 6 Mountain Lions and Humans

Mountain Lions in History: Native Peoples of North America

For many centuries prior to the arrival of Europeans, indigenous peoples of North America interacted with mountain lions. Cougars occasionally killed American Indians, and native peoples sometimes hunted and killed mountain lions.

Attitudes toward the cats varied from tribe to tribe. While most tribes held mountain lions in esteem, some peoples of the Pacific Northwest thought they were generally a mysterious, contemptible animal. Mountain lions were also viewed with suspicion by some tribes dwelling on the plains. In his book, *Red Hunters and the Animal People*, published in 1904, Charles Eastman recounts the attitudes of Sioux Indians (his ancestral people) toward various animals. The feelings are illustrated in one chapter as a conversation between an elder and younger men. In it the elder describes *igmutanka*, the cougar, in the following way: "They are unsociable, queer people. Their speech has no charm. They are very bashful and yet dangerous, for no animal can tell what they are up to. If one sees you first, he will not give you a chance to see so much as the tip of his tail. He never makes any noise, for he has the right sort of moccasins."

However, other tribes afforded the mountain lion great respect. The Hopi tribe, indigenous to the American Southwest, revered the mountain lion as a god and the protector of the tribe. An intriguing petroglyph (stone art) featuring a mountain lion was discovered in Arizona in 1934. Displayed at Petrified Forest National Park in Arizona, the rock art is thought to be around one thousand years old. It was created by the Anasazi, ancestors of the Pueblos.

Native hunters sometimes killed cougars. It was thought by many that ending the life of such a predator would mystically pass some of its spirit (and hence hunting skills) to the one who made the kill. Mountain lion claws and skins were used as adornments

This petroglyph of a mountain lion in Arizona is thought to be around one thousand years old. NPS Photo

by some tribes. Lewis and Clark recorded in their journals that some native peoples were very fond of mountain lion robes and noted it took the skins of four cougars to create such an article of clothing.

Numerous American Indian legends involve the mountain lion. One explains how the mountain lion came to have such a long, lean shape. A mountain lion, at the time a more stocky creature with a short tail, stole a meal of small rodents (variously identified as squirrels or prairie dogs) from Old Man, the creator. Old Man followed the mountain lion and caught it as it slept on a rock, gorged from its stolen dinner. He was so angry he stretched its husky body into a lean shape, also seizing and pulling its short tail into a long one in his anger. Ever since, the mountain lion has been a long, lean creature, ever in search of prey.

Mountain Lions in History: European Settlers in North America

European settlement in North America afforded the mountain lion the same fate as other larger predators. Farming cleared forests, depriving the cats of cover for hunting and rearing young, and also eliminated prey species such as deer and elk. Mountain lions sometimes preyed upon domestic livestock. Most settlers viewed them as a nuisance and threat to human life and livestock, and they sought to eliminate cougars from the landscape where possible.

Cleared land, previously forests, is estimated by some experts to have covered over 50 percent of the landscape in the eastern United States by 1850. In many locations the ratio of land converted from native woodlands to agricultural lands was even higher. The resulting loss of habitat for wild creatures, along with unregulated hunting, led to the rapid decline of both predators and ungulates alike. Historical records indicate mountain lions were essentially eliminated from most locations east of the Mississippi River by the close of the nineteenth century. The cats may have persisted longer in a few isolated locations, but the remnant population of Florida panthers is the only known population to persist until modern times.

The mountain lion ultimately fared better west of the Mississippi River, but not because settlers in that portion of the country looked more kindly upon the cats. Rugged, mountainous regions became strongholds for cougars after decades of deliberate extermination eliminated them from more accessible areas, especially where livestock was involved. By 1930, mountain lion populations were absent from most of their historic habitat in the United States.

The rapid plunge in mountain lion numbers from the late 1800s to 1930 was accelerated by government efforts to rid them from the landscape. Many states enacted bounties (payments for killing a certain type of animal) on mountain lions in response to the perception that cougars were dangerous to people and livestock. During the same period, the federal government employed professional hunters who attempted to eliminate mountain lions and other predators from federal lands.

In Montana, for example, a bounty on mountain lions was enacted in 1884. Interestingly, the original bounty offered for mountain lions (eight dollars) was eight times greater than that paid for an adult wolf (one dollar). A record 177 bounty payments were made for mountain lions in 1908. From 1925 to 1930, fewer than five bounty payments were made for mountain lions, though the bounty had increased to twenty-five dollars by 1930. Montana's bounty system for mountain lions was dropped in 1962. Records of the system from 1932 to its termination were lost, but some sources suggest fewer than five payments per year were made for mountain lions from 1932 to 1950, an indication of their scarcity. Mountain lion numbers began to increase in the state around 1950. One source indicates 167 bounty payments were made from 1961 to 1962, the final two years of the system.

Mountain Lions in Modern Times

The elimination of bounty payments and the enactment of legal protection of the mountain lion as a game animal that could be taken by hunters and trappers but not killed indiscriminately

A large cougar visits a water tank on the Sevilleta National Wildlife Refuge in New Mexico. Cougar populations expanded across much of their range in the final decades of the twentieth century. USFWS Photo

allowed cougar populations in western states to expand dramatically from 1950 to 2000. The early portion of this period also coincided with a rise in ungulate numbers in many locations in the West, a further boon to mountain lions. Experts believe mountain lion numbers in some areas in the Rocky Mountains may actually be higher at the present time than they were historically. Mountain lion populations surged during the late 1980s and 1990s in many places for reasons not fully understood. Cougar populations are thought to be stable or increasing in most regions of the West. Their future expansion into suitable habitat currently unoccupied will be dependent on human toleration for these notable carnivores.

Humans and Mountain Lions: Current Interactions and Challenges

The development of better techniques to census (estimate population numbers) mountain lions in recent years has contributed to refined estimates of local populations. However, one of the continuing challenges to mountain lion research and management involves the largely solitary and secretive nature of the big cats.

A mountain lion crosses the North Dakota Badlands at dawn. The future of this great cat depends on how much of the world humans are willing to share with this powerful predator. Licensed by Shutterstock.com

Mountain lions lured to suburban areas by deer and other prey dramatically increase the odds of human-cougar conflicts. Licensed by Shutterstock.com

COUNTERING A COUGAR ATTACK

At least two dozen fatal mountain lion attacks have been confirmed in North America since 1890. Other nonfatal attacks have also occurred. According to records compiled by the California Department of Fish and Wildlife, fourteen attacks happened in California from 1986 to 2014, three of which were fatal. Although mountain lions mauling humans is very rare (domestic dogs kill far more people on an annual basis than cougars), experts offer several pieces of advice on countering an aggressive encounter.

In most situations, mountain lions appear to ambush people in a predatory attempt, meaning the cougar plans to feed on its victim. If the animal perceives the person is not an easy meal, it will usually back off. Experts thus coach people to stand tall and spread their arms or raise them above their head to appear larger. Confronting the cat with eye contact and shouting is also advised. If sticks or stones are handy, hurl them at the cat or use a stout branch in self-defense. Back away slowly. Should the cat

In the past few decades, wildlife managers have witnessed booming deer (and in some cases elk) herds taking up residence in suburban areas in numerous locations. At the same time, development of land for human residence at or within the edges of rural wildlife habitat have increasingly found people and wild animals attempting to live together. These two factors, along with a growing mountain lion population, have led to dramatically rising numbers of human-cougar interactions in some areas. Mountain lions living at the edge of human society sometimes prey upon pets. They may be lured to suburban backyards and parks by robust numbers of ungulate prey. Such events dramatically up the odds of negative interactions between mountain lions and humans.

initiate physical contact, fight back. Blows to the end of the nose or a finger in the eye may convince the cougar to break the attack. Above all, do not turn your back to the mountain lion or run.

Most cougars that get into "trouble" with humans are sub-adults, many of which may have been orphaned by their mothers. These "teenagers" may not have learned from their mothers to distinguish domestic dogs or humans from wild prey and are essentially experimenting with new prey based on their lack of knowledge. Protecting female mountain lions with young may thus reduce the number of negative human-cougar interactions.

In mountain lion country, it's wise to hike with another person or in a group. Most mountain lion attacks are directed at a solitary human. Parents should also be aware that children make up a high percentage of cougar attack victims. Keep the family together when hiking or recreating in mountain lion country. Carrying pepper spray, the kind used by biologists and recreationists in bear country, is also an excellent preparation for deterring a cougar attack.

Cougars sometimes attack people in terrifying and occasionally fatal incidents. Increasing mountain lion numbers in some areas may also lead to a reduction of ungulate species highly valued by hunters, whose expenditures fund state wildlife agencies and contribute to many local economies. Currently hunting is the greatest single cause of cougar mortality in most western states where it is allowed. The extent to which mountain lions pose real threats to human safety, game populations, and livestock is not as thoroughly understood as many commentators (both pro- and anti-predator) suggest. Mountain lions are not endangered in the US, nor is the average citizen in any significant danger from a cougar. The extent to which *Puma concolor* is allowed to thrive in the future will depend as much on public perception as on scientific management.

Index

About the Author

Jack Ballard is an award-winning outdoor writer and photographer. In the past ten years his articles and/or photos have appeared in over twenty-five different regional and national magazines, including *Paddler* magazine, *Montana* magazine, *WildBird* magazine, *Colorado Outdoors*, *Birds & Blooms*, and others. He currently lives in Red Lodge, Montana.